THE SCHOOLS HISTORY PROJECT · S·H·P · OFFICIAL TEXT

w h a t   i s

history ?

Y 9

a *conclusion* to key stage 3

Ian Dawson

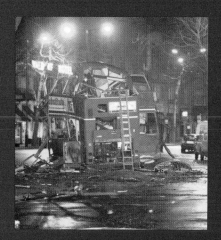

JOHN MURRAY

The Schools History Project

The Project was set up in 1972, with the aim of improving the study of history for students aged 13–16. This involved a reconsideration of the ways in which history contributes to the educational needs of young people. The Project devised new objectives, new criteria for planning and developing courses, and the materials to support them. New examinations, requiring new methods of assessment, also had to be developed. These have continued to be popular. The advent of GCSE in 1987 led to the expansion of Project approaches into other syllabuses.

The Schools History Project has been based at Trinity and All Saints College, Leeds, since 1978, from where it supports teachers through a biennial Bulletin, regular INSET, an annual Conference and a website (www.tasc.ac.uk/shp).

Since the National Curriculum was drawn up in 1991, the Project has continued to expand its publications, bringing its ideas to courses for Key Stage 3 as well as a range of GCSE and A level specifications.

This book is dedicated to Rob Phillips, inspirational colleague and good companion.

Acknowledgements

Written sources: p. 25 BMG Music Publishing Ltd.

Photographs: Cover & **p.i** Alastair Grant/Associated Press; **p.1** © Geoffrey Taunton; Cordaiy Photo Library Ltd./Corbis; **p.2** Alastair Grant/Associated Press; **p.3** © Reuters/Corbis; **p.4** *tl* © Bettmann/Corbis, *tr* © David Turnley/Corbis, *cr* © Corbis, *bl* © David Rubinger/Corbis, *br* © Corbis Sygma; **p.6** © Colchester Archaeological Trust; **p.8** Fotomas Index, Collection of Marquis of Salisbury at Hatfield House; **p.16** *l* & *r* EPA/PA Photos; **p.18** Mary Evans Picture Library; **p.19** *tl* popperfoto.com, *tr* The Pierpont Morgan Library/Art Resource, New York, *b* Private Collection/Bridgeman Art Library; **p.21** *tl* The Art Archive/Honourable Society of Inner Temple, London/Eileen Tweedy, *tr* Handschriften und Inkunabel Sammlung, Benediktinerabtei Lambach (Cod. Cml LXXIII f.64v & 72), *b* The British Library (ms. Roy.10.E.IV f.187); **p.22** *all* Mary Evans Picture Library; **p.23** *t* & *b* Mary Evans Picture Library; **p.25** Topham Picturepoint; **p.29** *t* courtesy Ian Dawson, *b* © Museum of London; **p.33** *tl* & *tr* Hulton Archive, *tcl, tcr, cl, c, cr* & *br* Mary Evans Picture Library, *bl* Science Museum/Science & Society Picture Library; **p.43** *Row 1 (from left)* British Library, London/Bridgeman Art Library, Musee d'Orsay, Paris/Giraudon/Bridgeman Art Library, © Bettmann/Corbis, Museo Archeologico Nazionale, Naples/Giraudon/Bridgeman Art Library, *Row 2 (from left)* © Corbis, Musée National du Château de Malmaison, Rueil-Malmaison/Bridgeman Art Library, © Massachusetts Historical Society, Boston/Bridgeman Art Library, The Stapleton Collection/Bridgeman Art Library, *Row 3 (from left)* © Flip Schulke/Corbis, © Bettmann/Corbis, Private Collection/Bridgeman Art Library, © 1990, Photo Scala, Florence, *Row 4 (from left)* © Louise Gubb/Corbis Saba, Museo Capitolino, Rome/Bridgeman Art Library, Pinacoteca, Sansepolcro/Bridgeman Art Library, Seattle Art Museum, Seattle/Giraudon/Bridgeman Art Library, *Row 5 (from left)* The Stapleton Collection/Bridgeman Art Library, © Bettmann/Corbis, © Bettmann/Corbis, © Gavin Wickham; Eye Ubiquitous/Corbis.

(t = top, b = bottom, l = left, r = right, c = centre)

While every effort has been made to contact copyright holders, the Publishers apologise for any omissions, which they will be pleased to rectify at the earliest opportunity.

© Ian Dawson 2004
First published in 2004 by
John Murray (Publishers) Ltd, a member of the Hodder Headline Group
338 Euston Road
London NW1 3BH

Layouts by Amanda Hawkes
Artwork by Art Construction, Peter Bull Art Studio, Jon Davis/Linden Artists, Richard Duszczak, Conny Jude, Tony Randell, Steve Smith
Cover design by John Townson/Creation
Typeset in Meridian by Fakenham Photosetting
Printed and bound in Italy by Printer Trento

A catalogue entry for this book is available from the British Library

Pupil's Book ISBN 0 7195 7966 X
Teacher's Resource Book ISBN 0 7195 7970 8

Introduction: History for the future

Before you finish Key Stage 3 here's your chance to look back at what you've learned and decide whether it's of any use to you! There's a lot here to think and argue about because History is a vital subject for improving your thinking!

Section 1

Section 1 (pages 2–17)
Can history help us deal with terrorism?

Find out whether the Romans, Queen Elizabeth I and the British army's experiences in Northern Ireland can teach us how to deal with terrorism today.

Section 2

Section 2 (pages 18–27)
Investigating ... history!

Put those historical skills and concepts to the test. Can they help you understand the history of one of today's hot topics of debate?

Section 3

Section 3 (pages 28–45)
What are your Top Five History Topics?

So what's been really significant? Decide which topics were the most important – or whether you should have done something else entirely!

This is the history that everyone ought to do!

Can history help us deal with terrorism?

Section 1

■ 1.1 What is terrorism?

Pages 2–5 are intended to get you thinking seriously about terrorism and deciding your own views before investigating three examples of terrorism from history.

1 Explain the two types of terrorism shown in Sources A and B.

2 Look at Sources A and B then make a list of other recent examples of terrorism. Which of the two types of terrorism are they?

3 What is the difference between a protester and a terrorist? For example, would you call a Greenpeace activist a terrorist or a protester for attacking a whaling ship to stop the crew catching whales?

▲ **Source A** This is one kind of terrorism. In this case the terrorists wanted to change the government of a country. They made a bomb which exploded in London. They hoped this would force the British government to change the government of Northern Ireland.

▼ **Source B** This is another type of terrorism. This time the terrorists wanted to change ideas, not a government. The bombers attacked a nightclub in Bali which was popular with tourists from Australia and the USA. They did this because they wanted to reduce the influence of non-Muslim countries on Indonesia.

4 How do you think terrorists such as those who planned the attacks in Sources A and B should be dealt with?

5 Can terrorism ever be justified? Give your reasons.

6 Can governments ever be terrorists? Give your reasons.

Terrorists – or freedom fighters?

How do you decide whether someone should be called a terrorist? Is it:

- what they do? (the **methods** they use)
- whether you agree with their **aims**?
- whether they are on the **winning** side or the **losing** side?

To help you think this through here are six individuals from the last 1000 years of history. Should any of them be called terrorists?

A Guy Fawkes

and the other Gunpowder Plotters wanted to change the country's religion back to Catholicism. They were caught in the act of trying to blow up King James I and Parliament in 1605.

B Menachem Begin,

leader of the Irgun, a Jewish group who blew up a hotel in Jerusalem in 1946. The explosion killed 88 people. The Irgun wanted the area around Jerusalem to be made into a country for the Jews. At the time the region was ruled by Britain. In 1948 the region was made into the Jewish country of Israel and Begin later became Prime Minister.

C Hereward the Wake, 1070.

Hereward wanted to force the Normans out of England. His men looted and set fire to the town of Peterborough, attacked Norman castles and killed Norman soldiers.

D Nelson Mandela.

Born in 1918, Mandela spent many years leading non-violent protests against white rule in South Africa. Eventually he decided that violent opposition was the only way to get his message across. His supporters sabotaged targets such as power plants and military bases but tried to avoid violence against people. He was imprisoned for life in 1962. Mandela was eventually released in 1990 and was elected President of South Africa in 1994.

E Richard Nixon,

President of the USA 1968–74. In 1973 Nixon wanted to get rid of the government in Chile (in South America). It had been democratically elected by the Chilean people but it had policies that the USA did not like. Nixon sent planes and other military aid to help rebels in Chile to overthrow the country's democratically elected government. The President of Chile and 3000 of his supporters were killed in the bombing and other attacks. Then a new, unelected government which agreed politically with the USA took over.

F Osama Bin Laden,

leader of the al-Qaeda terrorist network. In the 1980s he fought against the Russian takeover of Afghanistan because Russia would have banned the Islamic religion in Afghanistan. Later he declared war on the USA. His supporters destroyed the World Trade Center in New York on 11 September 2001 and have attacked other Western targets.

1 Who might have regarded each of these people as terrorists and why?

2 How else could their actions be interpreted?

3 Why do you get different interpretations of such people?

4 What can you learn from these examples about whether dealing with terrorism is simple or difficult?

5 Why do people turn to terrorism? Think about examples of terrorism that you have discussed in class or from your own knowledge. Which of these motives applied in each case?

- ◼ To end inequality
- ◼ Lack of power to influence events
- ◼ To improve people's lives
- ◼ To gain freedom
- ◼ Out of hatred or for revenge

6 What other motives can you think of?

How should governments deal with terrorism?

Here are two opinions that you will often hear when there is a terrorist attack anywhere in the world.

Never give in. Never negotiate with terrorists or listen to their complaints. The only way to end terrorism is to stamp out the terrorists, quickly and violently.

Deal with the causes. We need to listen to terrorists' demands and try to deal with their complaints. If we just kill or imprison terrorists and don't deal with the reasons for terrorism then more terrorists will soon appear.

7 In this section of the book your task will be to answer the following question: 'How should governments deal with terrorism?'

You are going to start with historical examples. Work in a pair or small group to research how governments have dealt with terrorist activity. There are three case studies on pages 6–14. Each group could focus on a different case study, or cover all three if there is time.

Your task is to make a short presentation (e.g. about three minutes long) which should include:

- ◼ three key pieces of advice for any government facing a terrorist threat
- ◼ historical examples to support your advice
- ◼ a conclusion that states which of the two speakers above ('Never give in' or 'Deal with the causes') you agree with – or whether you would take a different approach altogether.

Present your findings clearly and professionally – think about using a computer package like PowerPoint.

■ 1.2 Case study 1: How did the Romans deal with Boudicca?

Terror!

Britain in AD 61. Dead bodies lie in the streets. Houses burn until they are completely destroyed. The heads of murdered people are stuck on poles to terrify anyone who comes to see what has happened. The Roman historian Tacitus wrote 'The Britons took no prisoners. They wasted no time in getting down to the bloody business of hanging, burning and crucifying.'

Three towns, Colchester, London and St Albans, were destroyed in exactly this way. They had all been attacked and over-run by Queen Boudicca's army.

▼ **Source 1** A wall in Colchester destroyed by fire during Boudicca's revolt.

What did Boudicca want?

Boudicca was queen of the Iceni. She and her army used violence against the Roman invaders. The Romans had invaded Britain nearly twenty years earlier in AD 43. They wanted Britain's riches, which came from farming and mining silver and lead. Some local rulers, such as the king of the Iceni tribe in East Anglia, made peace with the Romans. However, when the king died, the Romans evicted Iceni nobles from their lands. Members of the royal family were treated like slaves. Queen Boudicca was flogged and her daughters raped.

That was when Boudicca hit back at the Romans for their treatment of her family. She may have wanted to push the Romans out of Britain but we do not know exactly what her aims were because the British did not keep written records.

Boudicca timed her attacks well. The Roman commander and his army were in north Wales. The towns that Boudicca attacked were poorly defended. Boudicca's army killed some Roman soldiers but most of the victims were ordinary Britons or retired Roman soldiers and their British families.

1 Why did Boudicca and her army attack the three towns?

2 Why were these attacks so threatening to the Romans?

3 Do you think these attacks can be called terrorism? Give your reasons.

How did the Romans respond?

Stage 1
The Roman commander, Paulinus, raced back from Wales and fought Boudicca's army in a battle. The Roman army was smaller but it won. Boudicca and her daughters committed suicide.

Stage 2
However, the Roman victory did not solve the bigger problem. Boudicca was dead but there were still many people who did not want the Romans in Britain. They might use terror campaigns just like Boudicca. How could the Romans stop more attacks?

The Emperor of Rome had to choose between two options:

Option 1 Suetonius Paulinus, the general who defeated the rebels.

Option 2 Julius Classicianus, a very experienced adviser but new to Britain.

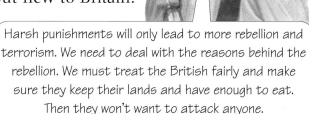

Never negotiate with terrorists. Stamp them out, quickly and violently. Destroy the homes and crops of all the tribes that rebelled. Punish their leaders severely. If we look weak there will just be more rebellion.

Harsh punishments will only lead to more rebellion and terrorism. We need to deal with the reasons behind the rebellion. We must treat the British fairly and make sure they keep their lands and have enough to eat. Then they won't want to attack anyone.

What would you recommend?

4 Which of the two options would you advise the Emperor to take, or would you suggest another option? Remember:

- Roman soldiers had been killed by Boudicca
- thousands of people had been killed in the towns destroyed by Boudicca
- the Romans wanted a secure and stable Britain in the future
- the Romans had a large Empire with lots of local groups who felt much like Boudicca
- no-one knew for sure what the results of either policy would actually be.

Your teacher can tell you what actually happened.

How should governments deal with terrorism?

Planning your advice

Now sum up the points that will help with the task on page 5.

5 Can you identify from this case study:
a) any important similarities with terrorism today?
b) any important differences from terrorism today?

6 What pieces of advice would you give for dealing with terrorism after investigating this historical example?

■ 1.3 Case study 2: How did Elizabeth I deal with terrorist threats?

Terror!

1570: assassination threat!
The Pope encouraged Catholics to assassinate Elizabeth. He said that Elizabeth was not the rightful Queen of England because she was a Protestant. He called Elizabeth 'a servant of wickedness' and said that 'whoever sends her out of the world not only does not sin but gains merit'.

1570s onwards: secret landings!
Catholic priests landed secretly in remote harbours. They were specially trained to spread the Catholic religion. Elizabeth and her councillors feared that they might include assassins and plotters.

▲ **Source 1** Elizabeth I, Queen of England 1558–1603. Some Catholics did not want Elizabeth to be queen because she was a Protestant and she had made the country's religion Protestant.

1583: a Catholic plot
A young Catholic called Francis Throckmorton made plans for a French army to invade England and replace Elizabeth as queen with her cousin, Mary, Queen of Scots, who was a Catholic.

1586: another plot!
Anthony Babington planned to rescue Mary, Queen of Scots, from prison and execute Elizabeth. Mary had fled to England after arguments with her lords in Scotland. Mary was kept in prison to prevent her leading a Catholic rebellion against Elizabeth.

1588: invasion!
Spain sent the Armada to invade England.

Why were the terrorists so dangerous to Elizabeth?

- ■ They had the support of the Pope
  - ■ . . . **and** Spain and France, both far more powerful than England
    - ■ . . . **and** there were many secret Catholics in England. They might support plots against Elizabeth but nobody knew exactly what they'd do
      - ■ . . . **and they had struck before!** In 1584 a Catholic had assassinated William of Orange, the leader of the Dutch Protestants.

1. Why did some people threaten Elizabeth?
2. Why were these threats so frightening?
3. Would you describe these threats as terrorism?

What were Elizabeth's options?

Elizabeth had to decide how to deal with the threats from plotters and assassins. Here is some of the advice she received:

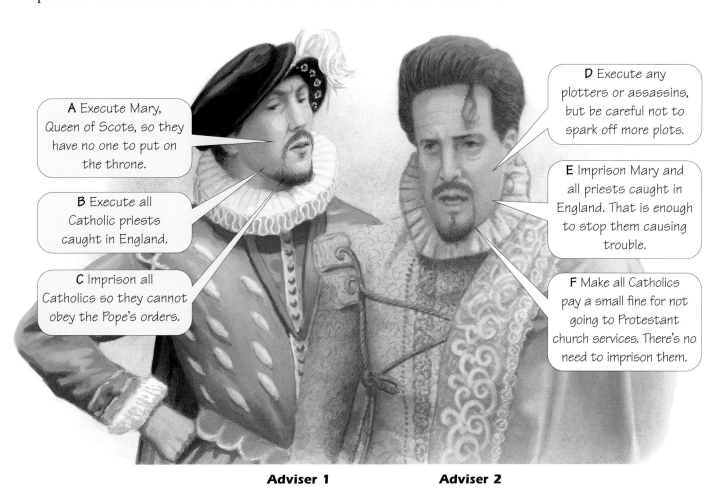

A Execute Mary, Queen of Scots, so they have no one to put on the throne.

B Execute all Catholic priests caught in England.

C Imprison all Catholics so they cannot obey the Pope's orders.

D Execute any plotters or assassins, but be careful not to spark off more plots.

E Imprison Mary and all priests caught in England. That is enough to stop them causing trouble.

F Make all Catholics pay a small fine for not going to Protestant church services. There's no need to imprison them.

Adviser 1   **Adviser 2**

What would you recommend?

4. Which of the two advisers do you agree with? Or would you suggest something different? Remember:

- ▪ it would be a terrible crime in the eyes of God to execute another queen
- ▪ you must try not to trigger an attack from France and Spain
- ▪ you must not appear weak
- ▪ you must not make 'moderate' Catholics hate you. Keep them on your side.

What did Elizabeth do – and not do?

1 Elizabeth set up a **spy network** to infiltrate groups of plotters and learn their plans.

2 Elizabeth made new **laws**:

- 1581: any priest holding a Catholic service and anyone attending it would pay a large fine and go to prison for a year
- 1585: Catholic priests were ordered to leave England within 40 days. Any found after that time would be executed.

However, ordinary Catholics were NOT rounded up and imprisoned.

3 Elizabeth ordered the executions of Throckmorton, Babington and other plotters. After 1585 Catholic priests were executed if they were caught.

4 Elizabeth **refused** to execute Mary, Queen of Scots. However, after the Babington plot, Elizabeth agreed to Mary going on trial for treason. Mary was found guilty and sentenced to death. Even then, Elizabeth delayed signing Mary's death warrant. Then, when she signed it, she refused to send it. In the end her councillors sent it and Mary was executed. Elizabeth was furious when she was told that Mary was dead.

(1) Why do you think Elizabeth chose each of these four policies?

Did Elizabeth's methods work?

A The plots continued throughout the 1570s and 1580s and priests continued to come to England in the 1590s.

B There was no support among English Catholics for the Spanish Armada. Ordinary Catholics did not want to rebel or replace Elizabeth.

C After 1588 there were no serious Catholic plots against Elizabeth.

D Elizabeth remained queen until she died in 1603.

E Two years after Elizabeth died, the Gunpowder Plotters tried to blow up James I and Parliament. Their aim was to make England Catholic again.

(2) Which of the results shown in the yellow box suggest that Elizabeth's policies worked? Which suggest that they did not?

▼ **Source 1** Part of a speech in Parliament in 1589 by Sir Christopher Hatton, one of Elizabeth's most important councillors.

Vile wretches, bloody priests and false traitors. We have chopped off some of the enemy's branches but they will grow again.

How should governments deal with terrorism?

Planning your advice

Now sum up the points that will help with the task on page 5.

(3) Can you identify from this case study:
a) any important similarities with terrorism today?
b) any important differences from terrorism today?

(4) What pieces of advice would you give for dealing with terrorism after investigating this historical example?

■ 1.4 Case study 3: How did the British tackle terrorism in Northern Ireland in 1971?

Terrorism and violence began in Northern Ireland in 1969 and continued for almost thirty years. During this period, which is known as The Troubles, over 3500 people were killed. This case study cannot fully explain **why** the violence began or look at all the attempts to stop it. It is far too complicated to cover in three pages. Instead we will focus on one of the most important periods in the struggle against violence.

Terror!

1969

10 people killed and 154 suffered gunshot wounds.

16 factories burned down,
170 homes wrecked,
24 Catholic pubs destroyed.

1970

26 people killed.

The Irish Republican Army (IRA) began a 'war' against the British army, killing British soldiers.

1971

186 killings, including 46 soldiers.

The IRA began a major bombing campaign, detonating 136 bombs by May. The targets were Protestant-owned shops and businesses.

What did the terrorists want?

Nationalists and Republicans want there to be one country of Ireland, independent from Britain.

- Nationalists are generally Catholic.
- The most extreme Nationalists are often called Republicans.
- The Provisional IRA (Irish Republican Army) strongly supports Northern Ireland breaking away from Britain and becoming part of the Irish Republic. It has often used violence against its opponents.

Unionists and Loyalists want to keep the union between Britain and Northern Ireland so that Northern Ireland remains part of The United Kingdom.

- Unionists are generally Protestant.
- The most extreme Unionists are often called Loyalists.
- The Ulster Volunteer Force (UVF) strongly supports Northern Ireland staying united with Britain. It has often used violence against its opponents.

1 Why did this terrorism take place?

2 Why did the terrorists see violence as justifiable?

3 If the terrorists thought violence was justifiable, why would this make it harder for the government to end the violence?

How did the British government deal with the terrorists in 1970–1971?

During these years the governments of Britain and Northern Ireland held many talks to try to find ways to end the terrorism. They also tried two other methods:

Method 1: they used the army to keep the peace

Date: August 1969

Place: The Bogside, a Catholic area of Londonderry

Events:

- Two days of rioting between Catholics and Protestants.
- Barricades and missiles made it impossible for the police to get into the area.
- At the same time there was rioting in Belfast. Houses were burned down. 1800 families were forced out of their homes. 1500 of them were Catholic.
- The police had lost control and there was a danger of the rioting spreading across Northern Ireland.
- The police were accused of bias in their harsh treatment of Catholics during the riots.

The choice: Should the British army be used to restore order – or should the government still use the police?

1 What arguments can you think of FOR and AGAINST using the army to restore order?

2 Decisions often have 'unintended consequences'. What does this phrase mean?

3 What was the unintended consequence in this case?

4 'Using the army was a poor decision because it made the violence worse.' Do you agree with this statement?

The government decided to use the army to restore order. The army was welcomed by the Catholic community at first ... but after the murders of four Protestants, the government ordered soldiers to search a Catholic area. This was against the army's advice. Suddenly the army looked like the enemy to many Catholics because tear gas was used to keep order and people were not allowed to leave their homes for 35 hours.

This helped the Provisional IRA win support. Up until this point the IRA had built up little support because it did little to defend the Catholic population. Now the IRA said it could defend the people – against the army.

Method 2: the army and police interned troublemakers

Terrorism and violence increased in 1971, despite the army being used to keep order. What should the government do?

Option 1 – take the army out of Northern Ireland and rely on the police to keep order.

**The aim –
to restore order and
stop the violence as
soon as possible**

Option 2 – use the army and police to arrest and then intern troublemakers. This method had worked against the IRA fifteen years earlier in 1956.

Option 3 – use the army and police to arrest troublemakers, put them on trial and then imprison them if they are found guilty.

The government decided to try internment (option 2). Internment means to imprison someone without trial.

The aim of internment was to wipe out the terrorist threat. Over 2300 people were interned but the information used to select them was out of date. None of the new Provisional IRA leaders was interned. Instead 1600 people were interned who were not involved in terrorism. There were other major problems too:

■ Only Republicans were interned. No Unionist paramilitaries were interned.

■ Torture and violence was used against some of the internees.

■ Bloody Sunday – on Sunday, 30 January 1972, 15,000 people joined a march against internment. It was organised by the civil rights movement. Trouble began when the army cordoned off the area and were then stoned by local youths. Shots were fired. Thirteen marchers were killed. All of them were unarmed. Some were shot in the back. There is still confusion over exactly why this happened. After this, support for the IRA increased further among some Catholics.

	Deaths in April–July 1971	**Deaths in August–November 1971**
Soldiers	4	30
Police (RUC/UDR)	0	11
Civilians	4	73

▲ **Source 1** Deaths before and after the start of internment in August 1971.

5 Why do you think the government decided to use internment instead of the other options?

6 Why did some people object to internment, even before it was used?

7 What were the unintended consequences of internment?

How did the governments bring peace to Northern Ireland?

The Troubles lasted for nearly thirty years. All the efforts by the governments of Britain and Ireland failed to end the terrorism in Northern Ireland. However, an agreement was finally reached in 1998. This was called the Good Friday Agreement. The Agreement came about because everyone involved **compromised** in order to get peace. You can see some of the compromises in the boxes below.

1 Can you match compromises A–E below to the groups, listed here, who made them? Note that some groups made more than one compromise. Choose from: **1** the British government; **2** the Irish government; **3** politicians in Northern Ireland; **4** Loyalist and Nationalist paramilitaries.

2 Why do you think compromise led to peace when using the army and internment did not?

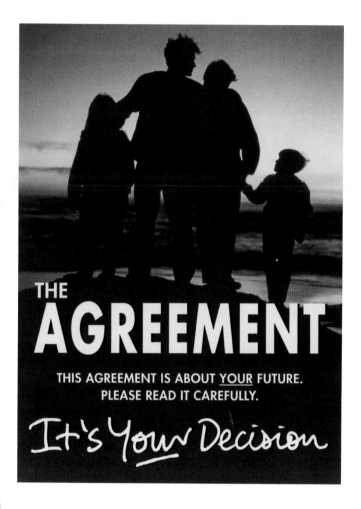

THE **AGREEMENT**

THIS AGREEMENT IS ABOUT <u>YOUR</u> FUTURE.
PLEASE READ IT CAREFULLY.

It's Your Decision

A Gave up its claim that Northern Ireland was really part of one country of Ireland

B Agreed to release paramilitary prisoners early

C Agreed to a ceasefire, ending the attacks and the killings

D Agreed to putting weapons out of action (decommissioning weapons)

E Agreed to a council containing politicians from all sides in Northern Ireland

How should governments deal with terrorism?

Planning your advice

Now sum up the points that will help with the task on page 5.

3 Can you identify from this case study:
a) any important similarities with terrorism today?
b) any important differences from terrorism today?

4 What pieces of advice would you give for dealing with terrorism after investigating this historical example?

The Big Ideas

Section 1

■ Can history help us deal with terrorism?

Yes, history can help deal with terrorism – but not by giving us easy answers. It's NOT a case of saying, 'This is what they did then so that's what we've got to do now.'

1 Here are three Big Ideas – lessons we can learn from the past. Can you finish off the speech bubbles so that they fit each Big Idea?

Big Idea 1   Simple solutions usually don't work …

Big Idea 2   … because decisions are always more complicated than they look at first glance …

Big Idea 3   … and because decisions can lead to completely unexpected results.

2 What can we learn from the way people have dealt with terrorism in the past? Here's one possible lesson. Do you agree with it?

'We need to deal with the causes of terrorism and treat ordinary people fairly to avoid creating more terrorists. If we just stamp out terrorists without dealing with the causes of terrorism then more terrorists will appear after a time.'

■ 1.5 Tackling terrorism today

▲ **Source 1** The aftermath of a Palestinian suicide bomb, Haifa, October 2003.

▼ **Source 2** Hanadi Darajat, the suicide bomber responsible for the explosion in Source 1.

On Saturday, October 4 2003, Bruriya Zer-Aviv was having lunch in a restaurant in Haifa with her son, his wife and their two children, Liran, aged four and Noya, a twelve-month-old baby. Then Hanadi Darajat walked into the restaurant and set off a bomb. Nineteen people were killed, including the whole Zer-Aviv family and the suicide bomber herself.

Read the information on these two pages.

(1) Why was the restaurant in Haifa bombed?

(2) How did Israel react and why?

(3) How is this event connected to what happened in 1948 (see page 17)?

(4) What can be done to stop this violence? Use these pages and what you have learned in Section 1 to give your answer.

Who's who and what do they want?

The **Palestinians** want their own, separate country for Palestinian Arabs and the return of the lands taken by Israel since 1948.

The **Israelis** want to keep the lands they have won since 1948 because they say these lands give them borders that are secure and defendable against enemies.

The **Palestinian extremists**, including Islamic Jihad, want to destroy and abolish the country of Israel. They say that the Jews have no right to a country in the region.

Key

▢ Lands taken by Israel since 1948

0   80 km

LEBANON
GOLAN HEIGHTS
Sea of Galilee
SYRIA
Beit She'an
Jenin
WEST BANK
Mediterranean Sea
Jerusalem
Dead Sea
GAZA STRIP
ISRAEL
JORDAN
EGYPT
SINAI PENINSULA
N
SAUDI ARABIA

▲ **Source 3** Israel's disputed territories.

Landmarks in the history of Palestine and Israel

Before 1948
This region was controlled by Britain. During World War One both the Arabs and the Jews thought that Britain had promised them their own independent country – on the same land.

1948
The United Nations said that there should be two new independent countries in the region, Palestine and Israel. Jewish settlers immediately created Israel and this led to war with neighbouring Arab countries who wanted to destroy Israel. Israel won the war, taking over most of Palestine. Over 500,000 Arabs fled or were forced out of Israel to live in refugee camps on the borders. The Darajat family fled their village of Beit She'an, which was taken over by Israel, and moved to the town of Jenin on the West Bank.

1967
In the Six-Day War, Israel defeated Egypt, Syria and Jordan. Israel took over the Golan Heights, the Sinai Peninsula, East Jerusalem and the West Bank. The town of Jenin was occupied by the Israeli army. Another 400,000 Arabs became refugees. One of the successful Israeli commanders was Ariel Sharon.

Bombings and peace talks
Terrorism increased after the 1967 war. The Palestine Liberation Organization (led by Yasser Arafat) and other, more extreme, Arab groups attacked civilian and military targets in Israel. This made peace talks difficult but in 1993 Arafat and the Israeli Prime Minister, Yitzhak Rabin, reached an agreement. Both said that the other people had a right to their own country. They were awarded the Nobel Peace Prize. Rabin vowed to pursue the peace process as if there was no terrorism, and to fight terrorism as if there was no peace process.

In 1995 Rabin was assassinated by a Jewish student angry at his concessions to the Palestinians.

In 2001 Ariel Sharon was elected Prime Minister of Israel because of his strong stance against terrorism. He ordered retaliatory 'collective punishment' against any families, villages and towns connected to terrorists acting against Israel.

In May 2003 undercover Israeli soldiers killed Fardi Darajat whom they said was a member of Islamic Jihad. Fardi's sister, Hanadi, became a suicide bomber in revenge for his death (see Sources 1 and 2). Until Fardi died, she had been a law-abiding law student.

Following the bomb attack, Israeli soldiers destroyed the Hanadi home in Jenin and the Israeli airforce attacked what they said were terrorist training camps in Syria. Syria threatened revenge on Israel for the air attack.

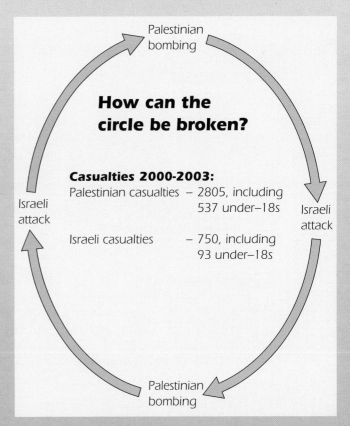

How can the circle be broken?

Casualties 2000-2003:
Palestinian casualties – 2805, including 537 under–18s
Israeli casualties – 750, including 93 under–18s

2 Investigating ... history!

Section 2

This section gives you the chance to show just how good you are at History by investigating ... what? Imagine you have just opened a box and found the pictures and sources on these two pages.

1 What topic do Sources 1–4 tell you about?

2 **a)** Put the sources in chronological order.
   b) When do you think the scenes in the sources took place? (Suggest dates or periods of history.)
   c) Discuss what clues or knowledge you have used to place the sources in chronological order and decide the dates.

3 Compile a list of good history questions to ask about this topic. Use the spider diagram as a guide.

4 What else can you learn from Sources 1–4? Look closely at the detail. Don't just think about the main topic but see what else you can find out from the sources too.

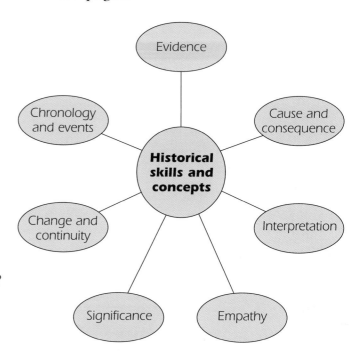

Evidence

Chronology and events

Cause and consequence

Historical skills and concepts

Change and continuity

Interpretation

Significance

Empathy

◀ **Source 1** Treadmills like this were used in prisons throughout the country. The theory was that sending people to prison was not a harsh enough punishment. Prisoners needed to do hard, boring work like turning the treadmill, as in this picture, or the crank, a machine fitted into cells where prisoners spent all day turning the handle a set number of times per hour.

▲ **Source 2** Crowds protesting against the execution of Ruth Ellis. Shortly after this photograph was taken, capital punishment (the death sentence) was abolished in Britain.

▶ **Source 3** This illustration shows the hanging of a gang of thieves who stole from a church. Churches were targets for gangs because of the church ornaments and money given for the care of the poor. Court Rolls record that a gang 'armed as for war' wounded the vicar at Stanford and stole goods worth £10.

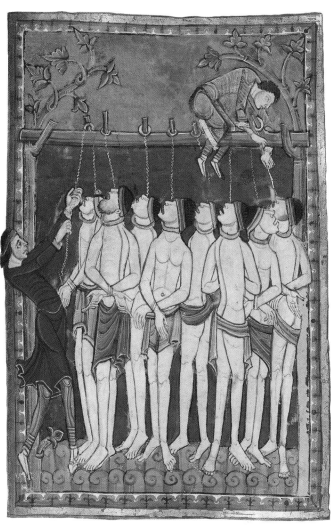

◀ **Source 4** At this time the normal punishment for vagabonds was whipping. For example, London watchmen caught John Allen, Elizabeth Turner and a group of others who had no work and were living as vagabonds. They were sentenced to be flogged severely and burnt on the right ear.

■ 2.1 Trials and punishments in the Middle Ages – were they cruel and bloodthirsty?

One of the most important skills in History is using sources as evidence. How good are your evidence skills?

Sources 1–4 come from the records of the royal courts held in Norwich in the early 1300s. Royal judges visited each county two or three times a year and every case they dealt with was briefly recorded.

▼ Source 1

Hamon, son of John in the Corner, was taken for stealing at night, one mare worth 10s and for stealing one horse worth 13s 4d and for robbing Thomas le Neve of goods worth 40s. He stands trial and is convicted. He is to be hanged.

Look at Sources 1–7.

1 Which of these sources would you use for investigating punishments?

2 Which of the sources would you use for investigating trials?

3 What can you learn from Sources 1 and 2 about punishments and the crimes they punished?

4 What can you learn from Sources 3 and 4 about attitudes to criminals?

5 'Drawings like Sources 5, 6 and 7 are not very lifelike, therefore we should just use documents like Sources 1–4 for investigating trials and punishments in the Middle Ages.' Explain why you agree or disagree with this statement, using one of the sources as an example.

6 'Trials and punishments were cruel and bloodthirsty in the Middle Ages.' Use the sources and captions to explain whether you agree with this statement.

▼ Source 2

Roger le Wodehird was taken for stealing a cow worth 5s. He stands trial and is found guilty. He is to be hanged.

▼ Source 3

John, son of Peter of East Lexham, was taken for the death of John Ballok. The jurors say that John Ballok was a thief and robbed Emma Rook of two sides of bacon. Emma raised the hue and cry after John Ballok. John, son of Peter, followed the hue and pursued John Ballok into a field. John Ballok drew a sword and wounded John, son of Peter. John, son of Peter, hit him on the head with a hatchet so that John Ballok died immediately. John, son of Peter, was returned to prison. The king was consulted and he was acquitted.

▼ Source 4

Peter le Synekere was taken for the burglary of the house of Godfrey of Gayton and for stealing half a bushel of wheat worth 14d, one tunic worth 10d and 3 hoods worth 8d. The jurors say that Peter stole the grain and other goods but they say that he did this because of hunger and destitution. He is returned to prison until consultations are made.

◀ **Source 5** A medieval illustration of a royal court, where serious cases were heard.

▲ **Source 6** Trial by ordeal. In the type of trial on the left, the accused had to carry a piece of red-hot iron for three metres. Her hand was then bandaged and unwrapped three days later. If God was saying she was innocent then her wound would be healing cleanly. However if the wound was not healing cleanly she was guilty. Trial by ordeal was only used when there was no evidence, such as in cases of murder when there was no witness.

▶ **Source 7** The stocks and pillory were used to punish people for minor crimes. The purpose was to humiliate offenders so that they would not break the law again and so that others would keep the law. London records give details of offences punished by being put in the pillory – selling 'stinking eels', 'selling oats, good on the outside, the rest bad', 'selling rings made of brass, plated with gold and silver as if they were gold and silver' and for 'lies uttered against the Mayor'.

■ **2.2 1770 – How was Mary Jones punished?**

In 1770 Britain was at war with Spain. Sailors were desperately needed for the navy and so press-gangs kidnapped any men they could find. One of their victims was Mary Jones's husband. Eighteen-year-old Mary was left with two children to look after. When she was unable to pay her rent she was turned out into the street. Alone in London, confused and desperate, she took a piece of cloth off a shop counter, realised the shopkeeper had seen her, and put it back. She had not stolen anything but the shopkeeper insisted on prosecuting her for theft.

(1) How do you think Mary was punished? Choose from Options 1–5 and explain the reasons for your choice.

Option 1: the pillory

The pillory was used for crimes such as selling underweight or rotten food or persistent swearing.

Option 2: whipping

Whipping was ordered for a wide variety of offences. Vagabonds were whipped, thieves who stole goods worth less than a shilling were whipped, and so were drunkards and anyone who regularly refused to attend church.

Option 3: prison

In the 1700s prisons were mostly used for debtors. Criminals were rarely sent to prison because transportation was the routine punishment.

Option 4: transportation

In the 1700s many criminals were transported to America. The punishment for theft was usually reduced from hanging to transportation for life; for example, Charles Scoldwell was transported for seven years for stealing two ducks. Transportation to America ended in 1775 but Britain then sent criminals to Australia until 1868.

Option 5: hanging

Between 1770 and 1830 an average of 140 people were hanged each year.

In 1815 225 crimes carried the death penalty, including:

- stealing horses or sheep
- pick-pocketing goods worth one shilling or more
- shoplifting goods worth five shillings or more
- being out at night with a blackened face
- sending threatening letters
- murder.

(2) Page 24 tells how Mary Jones was actually punished. Explain why the judge sentenced her to that punishment. Use Sources 1–5 to help you.

▼ **Source 1** The opinion of a leading churchman in the 1700s.

We need to prevent crimes and the best way is to frighten people away from crime with the most severe laws. Therefore as many crimes as possible should be punished with execution. The innocent may be hanged now and again but that is the price that must be paid for stopping crime. An innocent man who is hanged is dying for the good of his country.

▼ **Source 2** There were no police forces in the 1700s, just local watchmen. Criminals were not afraid of local watchmen, so the government tried to frighten people off committing crimes by making punishments very severe. However, criminals could not be punished if they were not caught – and most were not caught.

▶ **Source 3** In the 1700s and early 1800s people flocked to the growing towns to find work and wealth. However, many people remained poor, crowded together in bad housing and roaming the streets looking for work. In these large towns some people felt that nobody knew them and they could get away with anything.

▼ **Source 4** Pamphlets and broadsheets (newspapers) spread news of robberies and particularly lurid crimes which affected people's ideas about crime.

EXECUTION OF ALLEN, GOULD, & LARKIN,

At the New Bailey Prison, Manchester, on Saturday, November 23rd, charged with the Wilful Murder of Sergeant Brett, at Manchester, on September 18th, 1867.

the authorities, who had erected barricades about every thirty yards, and so prevented the great pressure that would have been. The prisoners were astir at an early hour, and partook of the holy communion, and at the appointed time. Calcraft, the executioner, was introduced, when the operation of pinioning was gone through. The prisoners the meanwhile showed wonderful confidence, and appeared to be the least concerned. They all shook hands together and affectionately embraced one another, and declared themselves ready. The mournful procession was then formed, and at once proceeded towards the scaffold, where on their appearance there was a slight manifestation of applause. Everything having been prepared, the ropes adjusted, the signal was given, and the unhappy men were launched into eternity. The prisoners appeared to die very easy.

▼ **Source 5** A graph showing the trends in crime, 1750–1900.

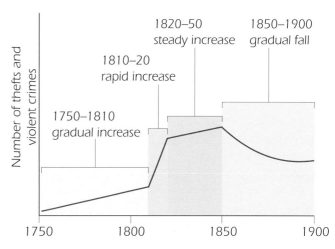

Number of thefts and violent crimes

1750–1810 gradual increase

1810–20 rapid increase

1820–50 steady increase

1850–1900 gradual fall

1750   1800   1850   1900

3 Read the information in the box below. Which of these three statements do you most agree with? Explain your choice.

   a) 'There was a complete change in punishments between 1770 and 1870.'

   b) 'There was a lot of change in punishments but some continuities between 1770 and 1870.'

   c) 'There was mainly continuity but also a little change in punishments between 1770 and 1870.'

4 Did severe punishments stop people committing crimes? Use the information on pages 22–24 to give your answer.

Punishments in the 1830s and after

In the 1820s and 1830s the government changed the punishments for many crimes.

- The pillory was abolished in 1837.
- Whipping was abolished for women in 1820 and for men in the 1830s.
- Crimes that had been punished by death were now punished by prison or transportation. By 1841 only murder and treason remained as capital crimes. An average of eleven people were hanged each year by the 1840s. The last public hanging was in 1868.

▼ **Source 6** The words of Sir William Meredith, an MP who wanted to reform punishments.
The Bloody Code and all the public executions do not deter criminals. If they did, would there be such crowds and laughter at executions? It is more important to have effective ways of catching criminals. If we increase their fear of being caught then they will think twice about committing the crime.

By 1860, over 90 per cent of serious offenders were sent to prison. The government took over the running of prisons. Men, women and children were separated, prisoners had to work and they spent long periods in silence. These methods were meant to help reform the prisoners.

Between 1829 and the 1850s police forces were formed all over the country. Politicians realised that harsh punishments were not stopping people committing crimes. People were less likely to commit crimes if there was a higher chance of being caught.

Mary Jones was hanged for theft. Normally, she would have been sentenced to death but her sentence would have been reduced to transportation. However, there had been a lot of shoplifting at the time of her 'crime' and the judge wanted to make examples of criminals to frighten other people away from crime. Mary was one of the 'examples' who were hanged.

2.3 'Let him dangle'

Nobody protested when Mary Jones was hanged but there were plenty of protesters in 1953 when Derek Bentley was executed …

Derek Bentley was nineteen when he was hanged for the murder of a policeman in 1953. Christopher Craig, the person who actually shot and killed the policeman, was aged sixteen but the law said that no-one under eighteen could be hanged. The prosecution claimed that Bentley had shouted 'Let him have it' to Craig. However, there was no definite proof that Bentley had said this. Even if he did say it, he could have been telling Craig to hand the gun over to the police. The jury recommended mercy but Bentley was hanged, despite his having learning difficulties and a mental age of ten. In November 1997, after a long campaign mounted by his family and friends, Bentley's case was referred to the Court of Appeal to re-examine the evidence. In 1998 the verdict of guilty was quashed.

▼ **Source 1** Derek Bentley's father and sister taking letters protesting against his execution to the House of Commons.

▼ **Source 2** Words from the song 'Let him dangle' by Elvis Costello.

Bentley said to Craig 'Let him have it Chris'
They still don't know today just what he meant by this
Craig fired the pistol, but was too young to swing
So the police took Bentley and the very next thing
Let him dangle
Let him dangle

Not many people thought that Bentley would hang
But the word never came, the phone never rang
Outside Wandsworth Prison there was horror and hate
As the hangman shook Bentley's hand to calculate his weight
Let him dangle

From a welfare state to society murder
'Bring back the noose' is always heard
Whenever those swine are under attack
But it won't make you even
It won't bring him back

Let him dangle
Let him dangle (String him up)

1. Why do you think Elvis Costello wrote this song?

2. Who might have a different view on whether it was right to execute Bentley and why?

3. If a songwriter thought that capital punishment was justified, what kinds of crime might he or she write a song about?

4. The story of Derek Bentley was made into a film. What would be the problems and advantages of interpreting this event in a film?

■ 2.4 Punishments through time

	THE EARLY MIDDLE AGES 400-1066	THE MIDDLE AGES 1066-1500	EARLY/MODERN BRITAIN 1500-1750	INDUSTRIAL BRITAIN 1750-1900	TWENTIETH CENTURY 1900-2000
Exile		Sanctuary		Transportation	
Reparation	Payments to victims				
Humiliation	Pillory and stocks				Community service
Custody	Slavery	Debtors' prison	Hard labour		Useful work
Fines		Fines			
Physical	Whipping	Mutilation			
Capital	Hanging	Burning at the stake / Beheading	Hung, drawn and quartered	Hanging in prison	Abolition of capital punishment

TYPES OF PUNISHMENT

1 a) Which change in the history of punishments do you think was the most significant?
  b) Explain what criteria you used to decide your answer to 1a).

2 Why might other people have different opinions about which change was the most significant?

3 Which two illustrations or sources on punishments through time (pages 18–25) would you choose if you were asked to:
  a) design a display board for a new museum called The Dungeon of Horrors
  b) write a page about punishments in the 1700s and 1800s for a Year 8 textbook
  c) write an article on changes in punishments for a serious newspaper.

Explain the reasons for your choices.

4 Split into groups of four. Two people in each group believe that the death penalty should be re-introduced. The remaining two believe that it should not be re-introduced. Spend five minutes in your pairs finding evidence from this timeline and pages 18–25 to support your view, then discuss in your groups whether the death penalty should be re-introduced.

5 Do you think you can learn anything from the history of punishments to help you understand punishments today?

The Big Ideas

Investigating history

Over the last few pages you have been investigating the history of punishments. To do this, you have been using your historical *skills* and your understanding of historical *concepts*. This activity gives you the chance to sum up what you have learned about 'doing history' so far.

1 Which historical concept is each of the questions below dealing with?

2 What three pieces of advice would you give each set of pupils to help them answer their question well? You don't have to give the answers, dates or any historical information. You need to tell them how to answer questions dealing with the concepts.

What are your Top Five History Topics?

Over the last three years you have investigated lots of history. All of it was chosen for you. The government decides what topics go into the National Curriculum and teachers have a little freedom to add topics of their choice – but what do *you* think everyone should study in History in years 7, 8 and 9? That's your final task. You can choose FIVE topics, of which at least one must be European or World history. You must choose:

- one **event**
- one **person**
- one **theme** through time
- and **two** other topics – people, events, themes, it's up to you.

Remember, at least one of these must be non-British history.

You could make a poster showing your choices, like the one opposite that shows my five choices.

Pages 28–44 will help you to make your choices. They'll remind you of some of the main topics you've studied and mention some that you haven't. Most importantly, you need to think about SIGNIFICANCE. Are some people and events more significant than others, and how do we decide?

The cartoons below provide some clues about the kind of criteria you could use to decide which people and events are the most significant.

1 Can you work out what these criteria are from the clues?

2 Can you think of any other criteria?

3 Are any of the criteria more important than others?

1

2

3
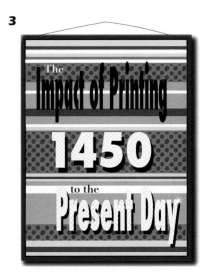

Ian Dawson's choice

My Top Five History Topics

▬ One event: The Black Death

I chose this event because it dramatically affected everyone who was alive at the time and it continued to affect the way people lived for centuries afterwards. The Black Death was a true disaster, but it led to real improvements in living standards and great developments like printing, and then on to other new ideas that changed the world. It's exciting working out the links across hundreds of years and it's a reminder that we can never be sure how things are going to work out.

▬ One theme: The fight for the vote from the Middle Ages to the present

This girl was a suffragette who was imprisoned a hundred years ago for demanding votes for women. I like this photo because she doesn't look like someone from history. She could be a student today.

I wonder what happened to her? The photo reminds me how ordinary people faced dangers to win the rights we have today – the villagers who rebelled in 1381; the soldiers who fought for Parliament in the Civil War; the workers at Peterloo.

4 Can you work out which criteria I used to choose these topics?

▬ One person: Mahatma Gandhi

What do you do if you hate the way that a government discriminates against some of its people, because of their colour or religion or sex? Gandhi protested but he never used violence. His peaceful campaigns changed the way India was governed and they inspired people all over the world. He was quite simply a wonderful example of how to treat other people with dignity and kindness.

And two other topics:

▬ The medical revolution

Twenty years ago my life was saved by complex surgery. I think the medical revolution (changes in surgery and public health) is the most important change in the last 100 years because it's saved and improved the lives of so many people. Average life expectancy has gone up since 1900 from 45 to nearly 80!

▬ The rise of Hitler and the way ordinary people fought him

My first reason for choosing this topic is that it shows us that evil men can take control in any country. If people are desperate they will vote for someone who gives them easy answers to their problems. Secondly, ordinary people like my dad and mum (and millions more like them) joined the forces to fight Hitler. So too did people all over Europe and in the USA, Australia and many other countries. We should remember the sacrifices of ordinary people who risked everything to stop evil.

3.1 Famous events – but which were the most significant?

This is where I start helping you choose your Top Five History Topics. You need to include at least one event, like those shown on this timeline and on pages 32–33. The timeline will remind you of some of the big events in British history.

The most significant events in British history

Event	My reasons for thinking these events were **really** significant
1	
2	
3	

The timeline shows some famous events in British history.

① What criteria would you use to work out which events were the most significant? The speech bubbles on the timeline will help you.

② **a)** Can you think of any significant events that have been missed off the timeline?

b) What would you put in a speech bubble to summarise the importance of each of these events?

③ When you have looked at pages 32–33, fill in a copy of the table above with the events that you think were the most significant.

Over 40 per cent of Britain's population died of the Black Death but it led to everyone becoming free and introduced improvements to everyday life that lasted for hundreds of years.

The Black Death and Peasants' Revolt

AD 1530

The first professional sports leagues

By the 1880s we could watch the Football League and the county cricket championship. Professional sport gave us a completely new kind of entertainment.

← AD 1860

Discovering the cause of disease

In 1860 Louis Pasteur first suggested that germs cause disease. This led to inoculations and antiseptics and to improved health for millions.

← AD 1880

AD 1928

VOTES FOR

In 1928 all men and women over the age of 21 were given the vote for the first time. This led to new laws and reforms that still affect everyone's lives today.

BALLOT BOX

Votes for all

Magna Carta

The barons forced King John to agree to rules about how he governed the country. This didn't include letting ordinary people having a say in government.

← AD 1215   ← AD 1066   AD 600   AD 43/BC

The Norman Conquest

We conquered England. We became the new rulers and built castles to protect us from the English.

The Anglo-Saxon invasions

We brought the language you still use today. We were the first English people.

The Roman Conquest

We built roads and baths and influenced the way Britons lived for 400 years.

AD 1415 →

The Battle of Agincourt

Henry V and his archers won a great victory over the French. This led to England ruling parts of France for the next 40 years.

The Reformation

New religions developed. All the monasteries were closed which hurt the poor. Some people were executed because they opposed the changes.

AD 1534

The English navy stopped the Spanish invasion fleet, the Armada.

The defeat of the Spanish Armada

AD 1588 →

The Civil War

We executed the king. Parliament ruled the country for ten years before there was a new king. This began to change ideas about who should govern the country.

AD 1649

← AD 1805

The battles of Trafalgar and Waterloo

In 1805 Nelson beat the French navy and stopped France invading Britain. In 1815 Wellington's British army beat Napoleon's French army and ended over twenty years of war.

← AD 1780

The Industrial Revolution

Instead of working on farms, people like us moved to towns. Our lives were very different in the crowded towns where there were lots of new inventions such as railways.

← AD 1776

The American War of Independence

Britain's American colonies won their independence and created the USA.

Great inventions – would you rather have a computer or a bar of soap?

On pages 30–31 you looked at some very famous events. They were mostly about politics, but what about a different kind of event – inventions? How would we all get on without electricity or flush toilets? Perhaps they should be in your Top Five History Topics . . .

1 Match the inventions on this page to the people opposite who played a key part in developing them.

2 Can you think of any other important inventions that ought to go into this list?

3 What criteria will you use to decide which inventions were the most significant? Look back to the cartoons on page 28 for ideas.

4 Can you think of any reasons why people might disagree about which inventions were the most important?

5 Now complete question 3 on page 30, choosing your three most significant events.

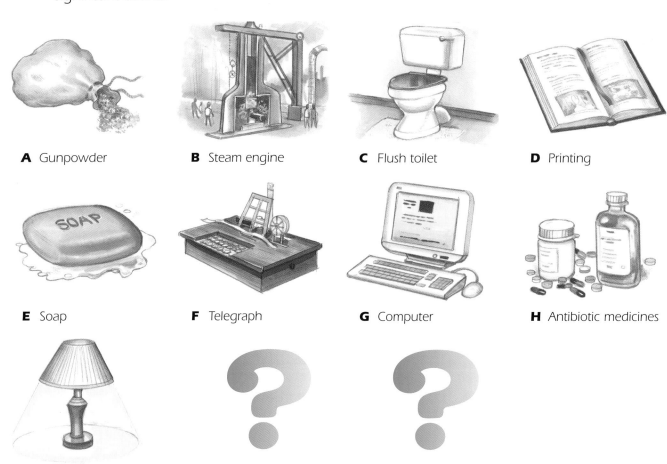

A Gunpowder   **B** Steam engine   **C** Flush toilet   **D** Printing

E Soap   **F** Telegraph   **G** Computer   **H** Antibiotic medicines

I Electricity

Remember me every time you press a switch. My discoveries in the 1830s led to more inventions, by people like Thomas Edison.

1 Michael Faraday

My machine was the first one in Europe in the 1450s.

And I brought this discovery to England in the 1470s.

2 Johannes Gutenberg and William Caxton

In the 1760s I made these machines more powerful. They revolutionised all kinds of industries and how people travelled.

3 James Watt

This discovery had been used in China but I was the first to describe it in Europe, in 1252.

4 Roger Bacon

In the 1820s I started work on my calculating machines, which finally changed people's lives over 150 years later.

5 Charles Babbage

I became famous in the 1880s for making these. Some ladies fainted when they saw one in my shop window!

6 Thomas Twyford

My discovery has saved millions of lives since World War Two.

7 Alexander Fleming

In 1776 it took six weeks for news of the American Revolution to reach London. Our invention in the 1840s sent news instantly, leading to other developments such as the telephone and radio.

8 William Cooke and Charles Wheatstone

This invention has been used for thousands of years but it often damaged the skin. I developed a new type in the early 1800s that did not damage skin and I sold it cheaply so that ordinary people could buy it.

9 Andrew Pears

■ 3.2 Which theme through time will you choose?

You must include one *theme* through time in your Top Five History Topics. This page shows you an example of what I mean by a theme. It is the theme I chose for my own top five – the theme of medical progress.

When did people's health improve?

The Romans built sewers and piped fresh water into towns. However, no-one knew what caused diseases. Average lifespan – 40.

In the Middle Ages illnesses were treated with herbal remedies. Doctors bled patients when the stars were in the right part of the skies. There were no cures for diseases because people did not understand what caused them.

| 500BC | 0 | AD500 | AD1000 | AD1500 |

1 **a)** Can you spot any continuities on the timeline up to the 1800s?
   b) Why was 1860 an important date in this story?
   c) When did the most rapid changes happen?

2 Summarise the whole story of medical progress in four or five sentences.

3 Which event do you think was the most significant in this story?
Explain your choice.

4 Do you think that this theme is significant enough to include in your
Top Five History Topics? Explain your decision.

5 Is there anything you can add to bring this story up to date?

Edward Jenner discovered how to vaccinate people to stop them catching smallpox. However, nobody knew how to make this technique work to stop other diseases.

In the 1500s the invention of printing spread ideas. Doctors experimented to learn more about anatomy and about how the body works. In 1628 William Harvey discovered how blood circulates round the body. However, these discoveries did not actually make people healthier. Average lifespan – 40.

In 1860 Louis Pasteur suggested that bacteria (germs) cause disease. Then other scientists discovered ways of preventing people catching diseases. This led to the first antiseptics which killed germs. All these developments convinced governments that they needed to clean up towns, improve housing and give people fresh water and sewerage systems. Average lifespan by 1900 – 50.

In the early 1900s the elderly were given old-age pensions and the unemployed received benefits. Schoolchildren had their health checked.

The first antibiotics were developed during the Second World War. Penicillin had been discovered by Alexander Fleming years earlier. Once governments realised that penicillin could save their soldiers, they paid for the production of penicillin and many other antibiotics.

The National Health Service started in 1948. For the first time everyone could get free medical treatment. Average lifespan by 2000 – well over 70.

AD1600   AD1700   AD1800   AD1900   AD2000

35

More themes to choose from!

Perhaps you don't think the story of health and medicine is important enough to be one of your Top Five History Topics. Here are some more themes for you to think about.

1 How would you bring each theme up to date?

2 Which of these themes do you think is the most significant? (Remember to work out your criteria before you start discussing this.)

3 What other themes have you studied in History?

4 Which theme will you choose for your Top Five History Topics – and why?

1 The story of . . . how we won the vote

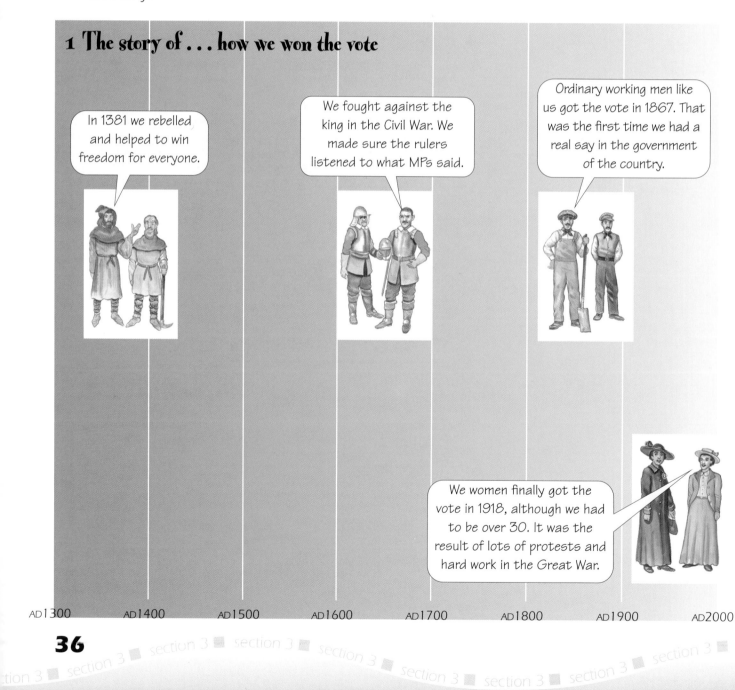

In 1381 we rebelled and helped to win freedom for everyone.

We fought against the king in the Civil War. We made sure the rulers listened to what MPs said.

Ordinary working men like us got the vote in 1867. That was the first time we had a real say in the government of the country.

We women finally got the vote in 1918, although we had to be over 30. It was the result of lots of protests and hard work in the Great War.

AD1300　　AD1400　　AD1500　　AD1600　　AD1700　　AD1800　　AD1900　　AD2000

2 The story of . . . enjoying ourselves

We've got some spare time so we're going to . . .

tell stories about battles and giants

or play music and dance

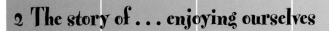

go to the theatre

or to see the bear baiting at the fair

go to watch a match

or sing songs round the piano

go to the cinema

or listen to the radio

AD1300　　　AD1400　　　AD1500　　　AD1600　　　AD1700　　　AD1800　　　AD1900　　　AD2000

3 The story of . . . getting there faster

How quickly can you get this letter from London to Edinburgh?

About ten or twelve days, but quicker if it's important news and I get fresh horses.

Eleven days. It's slow going in a coach on these terrible roads.

Less than a day. You won't get faster than that!

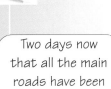

Two days now that all the main roads have been improved so much.

AD1300　　　AD1400　　　AD1500　　　AD1600　　　AD1700　　　AD1800　　　AD1900　　　AD2000

4 The story of . . . making ourselves comfortable

What I like best about our home is . . .

iron locks on the door and window frames, and a separate room to sleep in.

having two floors and separate rooms.

our own water pipes and a toilet in our yard that we don't have to share with the rest of the street.

electric lights in all the rooms, and a refrigerator and washing machine.

AD1300　　　AD1400　　　AD1500　　　AD1600　　　AD1700　　　AD1800　　　AD1900　　　AD2000

■ **3.3 Great Britons – who was the greatest of them all?**

You need to include at least one *person* in your Top Five History Topics. After all, History is all about people. You learn far more about people in History than you do in any other subject. In 2002 the BBC held a competition called 'Great Britons'. People voted for the person they thought was the Greatest Briton in history. The top three were Winston Churchill, Isambard Kingdom Brunel and Diana, Princess of Wales. Do you agree with that list? Who would you choose as the three Greatest Britons of all time and would you include any of them in your Top Five History Topics?

1 Complete the missing speech bubbles. Some of them contain a couple of clues but you will have to work out the others for yourself! Remember to say in the speech bubble why the person was significant.

2 Who else would you add to this list and what would you write in their speech bubbles? Look at pages 32–33 for ideas.

3 What criteria would you use to decide which people were the most significant?

4 Who would you choose as the three most significant Britons of the last 2000 years?

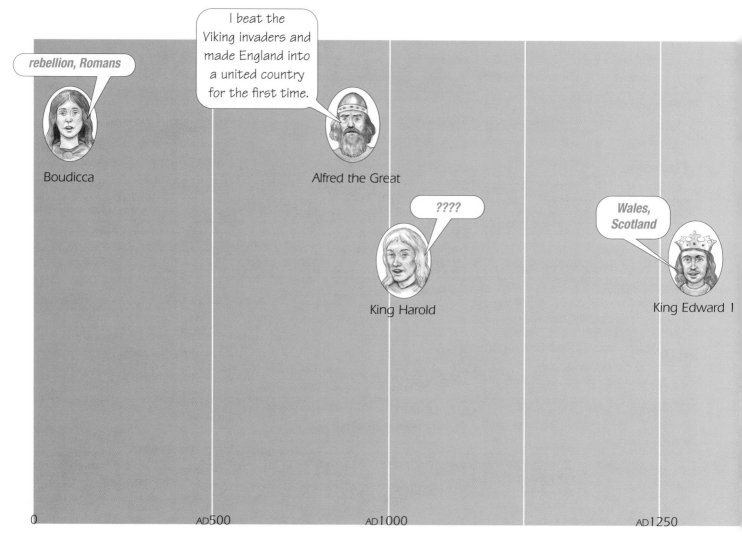

And what about us? You don't know our real names but we campaigned to get better lives for everyone. Thanks to us, you are all free and can vote and have equal rights. That's very important. Why don't you put 'The Unknown Campaigners' on your list of Great Britons?

The peasant rebels of 1381

The Levellers

The Chartists

The Suffragettes

5 The people in your class have probably made different choices. Why are there disagreements? Can you see any patterns in the choices, for example do girls differ from boys?

6 Some people are famous but they are not significant. Can you think of any examples of people who are famous but not significant?

????

King Henry V

I founded the Church of England because I needed a son. If anyone opposed me I had them executed.

King Henry VIII

????

William Shakespeare

????

Oliver Cromwell

I was the first European person to sail to Australia and I set up the first links between Europe and many other countries.

James Cook

Trafalgar, France

Horatio Nelson

????

Emmeline Pankhurst

People still read my books 200 years after I wrote them.

Jane Austen

slavery

William Wilberforce

My ideas were used to set up the National Health Service.

William Beveridge

railways, bridges

Isambard Kingdom Brunel

????

Winston Churchill

AD1500

AD1750

AD2000

■ 3.4 The history of the world – in a day!

By now you should have some idea of who or what will be your person, event and theme for your Top Five History Topics. But it's not quite time yet to make your final decision. We have concentrated on British history so far because the National Curriculum says that everyone has to study British history at Key Stage 3. Everyone does some world history too but, because schools choose their own topics, students do all kinds of different topics – anything from America or India, Africa or China. Before you choose what YOU think everyone should study you need to look at world history as well as British history. You might want to choose some world history events, people or themes for your top five. At least one of your choices must be a non-British topic. Of course you could decide to include three or four non-British options. That would be up to you.

1 Imagine that the history of the human race could be fitted into just 24 hours. The first people walk on earth at midnight and our lives are taking place at midnight 24 hours later. You can see some of the main events in world history in the pictures on the right. At what time in the 24 hours is each one happening?

2 Can you think of any other major events or discoveries that ought to go into this summary of world history?

3 Divide the class into ten groups, one for each square on these two pages. In turn each group should explain to the rest of the class why the event in their square is significant.

1 25,000 years ago the first people walked the earth. They lived as hunter-gatherers, following the herds of animals as the seasons changed.

2 Slowly people started to settle down to live in one place. They were the first farmers, sowing seeds and herding cattle.

5 New religions developed – Buddhism, Christianity and, later, Islam. The Roman Empire ruled most of Europe and North Africa.

8 The Industrial Revolution started in Britain, then spread round the world. Steam, iron and electricity transformed many people's lives.

3 The wheel, the plough and pottery were invented. People began living in towns and trading with each other.

4 The pyramids were built in Egypt. Writing was used for the first time for communication. Stonehenge was built.

6 In the period known as the Renaissance, thinkers challenged old ideas and made new scientific discoveries, such as Copernicus's theory that the Earth moves round the Sun, not the Sun round the Earth.

7 Explorers from Europe travelled to America, Africa and to Australasia. They wiped out most of the native peoples with their diseases and wars.

9 The First World War broke out, followed just twenty years later by another world war.

10 The first atom bomb was dropped, threatening people with worldwide destruction.

■ 3.5 The most significant people in the history of the world?

(1) The information below tells the stories of two of the famous people on page 43. Who are these two people?

(2) Using a copy of the Significance Grid below, give mystery people A and B a score out of 4 (4 = very significant, 0 = not significant at all) for each criterion and add up their total scores.

(3) Research the rest of the people on page 43 and complete a copy of the grid for each one.

(4) Compare the totals. Who are the three most significant people in world history?

(5) How many reasons can you think of why people would disagree about the choice of the most significant three?

Criteria	Score
1　How long-lasting was his/her influence?	
2　Did he/she play a vital part in events at the time he/she lived?	
3　Was his/her influence truly worldwide?	
4　Your choice of other criteria	

Mystery person A

1 He was a great soldier.

2 He recaptured Jerusalem, one of the holy cities of his religion, from the Crusaders. No Christian army entered Jerusalem for over 700 years after he won it back.

3 Even Richard the Lionheart could not recapture Jerusalem from him.

4 He was generous to his enemies. A Christian churchman wrote 'He sent men out of Jerusalem to greet the Bishop of Salisbury and his party of pilgrims. He asked the bishop to stay in his palace and entertained him at his own expense, giving him many gifts'.

5 One of his supporters wrote 'He could recite by heart the histories of the Arab tribes. Those who sat with him learned things they would never have learned elsewhere.'

Mystery person B

1 He was born and educated in India but studied law in England.

2 He worked as a lawyer in South Africa, fighting against racial discrimination.

3 His simple life and methods of non-violent protest inspired people all over the world, including those in the USA and South Africa.

4 He led the successful campaign to win independence for India from British rule.

5 A Prime Minister of India said 'What stood out was how well he got on with all kinds of people. He became a link between the poorest peasant, whom he always sought to help, and princes and rich industrialists. He was certainly the greatest individual I came across in my life.'

Saladin
(died 1193)

Louis Pasteur
(died 1895)

Mahatma Gandhi
(died 1948)

Alexander the Great
(died 323BC)

Adolf Hitler
(died 1945)

Napoleon Bonaparte
(died 1821)

George Washington
(died 1799)

Abraham Lincoln
(died 1865)

Martin Luther King
(died 1968)

Mao Zedong
(died 1976)

Karl Marx
(died 1883)

Leonardo da Vinci
(died 1519)

Nelson Mandela

Homer
(died c. 750BC)

Jesus Christ
(died c. 29AD)

Muhammad
(died 632)

Genghis Khan
(died 1227)

Franklin Delano Roosevelt
(died 1945)

Marie Curie
(died 1934)

Mother Teresa
(died 1997)

The Big Ideas

So what **should** everybody learn about in History?

You should now have decided on your Top Five History Topics.

I don't expect that you agree with all my five choices on page 29. Everyone in your class has probably made different choices.

Everyone has a different idea about what is significant in history.

That is the Big Idea for this section.
Here are some reasons why.

1 Think about the questions attached to the boxes below.

2 What other reasons can you think of?

Interests
Someone particularly interested in science might choose a scientific invention as their 'event'.

How did your personal interests affect your choice?

Race or nationality
Somone from a country other than Britain might choose fewer British topics.

How might your choice be different if you lived in or came from a different country?

Political views
Someone who thought Britain should be a republic not a monarchy might be less likely to pick a king or queen as their 'person'.

What kind of political views affected your choices?

Audience
You were choosing topics to be studied in school.

How would your choice be different if you were making a TV series and wanted to get a big audience?

Impact
Most people choose events, people or themes which have impact. But impact is hard to judge.

Do you think that impact on a large number of people over a short amount of time is less or more significant than impact on a small number of people over a long period? Why?

Not knowing enough history
If someone only knows about the last hundred years they would probably choose Churchill as a significant person because he led the fight against Hitler. But in the big picture is that any more important than Wellington and Nelson beating Napoleon; or the English navy defeating the Spanish Armada or Alfred the Great beating the Vikings?

Did anybody else choose a topic that you don't know anything about?

... or possibly ...

Knowing too much history!
Some people become such experts in just one topic from history that it is all they think about. To them it is all important. They can't see why others disagree.

Did you put in your 'expert' topic? What was it and why are you so interested in it?

And finally . . .

Don't forget how much you have learned and discovered in History. Here are just a few of the questions you have been able to answer! Can you add any more to this list?

Have you done too much or too little modern history?

Would you like to have studied more local history?

Why did the Normans win the battle of Hastings?
Does everybody agree that King John was a terrible king?
What was it like to live in a castle in the Middle Ages?
Was the Black Death really so important?
How do we know about life in the Middle Ages?
Why was printing such an important invention?
Why did Henry VIII shut down all the monasteries?
How do we know about Queen Elizabeth I?
What was it like to fight in the Civil War?
Why did Oliver Cromwell turn down the chance to be king?
Did the British Empire improve people's lives in India?
What kinds of sources tell us about life during the Industrial Revolution?
Were the suffragettes heroines?
What was it like to be a soldier in the trenches?
Why did World War Two begin?
Why was the Holocaust so important?
How do we evaluate sources to find out the truth about what happened in the past?

Have you done enough history covering other parts of the world?

Would you like to have studied more prehistoric or ancient history?

Have you spent too much time on wars and not enough on the way people live? Or perhaps it's the other way around?

Index